AUSTRAL
RED CENTRE

Photography by Geoff Higgins
Text by Dalys Newman

WOOLLAHRA

PRECEDING PAGE: Stunning vistas in the heart of the Channel Country, near Windorah in Queensland.

ABOVE: Mount Chambers Gorge in the Flinders Ranges. Forming South Australia's most extensive mountain chain, these ranges are a series of long parallel ridges separated by narrow valleys and wide alluvial plains.

BELOW LEFT: Free-standing sandstone cliffs, part of the James Range in Rainbow Valley, glow in the afternoon sun when the rainbow-like rock bands are highlighted. In earlier wetter climates, the red iron of the sandstone layers dissolved and evaporated to the surface during the dry season. Red minerals formed a dark, iron-rich surface layer with the leached white layers below.

BELOW RIGHT: The abandoned Cadelga outstation in South Australia dates back to 1878. In the 1930s it was used as an observation post by the Royal Geographic Society for the transit of Venus.

OPPOSITE: The Gammon Ranges National Park in South Australia's far north is a wilderness area of deep gorges, rocky plains, steep mountains and stony rivers. It was home to the Adnyamathanha people who have left a legacy of rock paintings and carvings in the area.

OPPOSITE: Remains of mines, old miner's camps and stone buildings are preserved at Arltunga Historic Reserve, east of Alice Springs. The police station and gaol have been restored and house a museum and visitor's centre. Once a booming goldrush town and Central Australia's first official township, Arltunga was born out of a gold strike in 1887.

ABOVE: Outback scenery at the James Range, south-west of Alice Springs.

CENTRE: Old stock yards at the Arkaroola Homestead in the rugged northern Flinders Ranges just to the east of the Gammon Ranges National Park. Arkaroola is a 61 000 hectare privately owned wildlife sanctuary.

RIGHT: Camerons Corner, named after surveyor John Cameron, stands at the junction of New South Wales, Queensland and South Australia. Here, too, is the Dingo Fence, built originally in the 1880s and maintained to keep dingoes out of the sheep-grazing areas of New South Wales. The longest fence in the world, it runs from Queensland down to the cliffs of the Great Australian Bight.

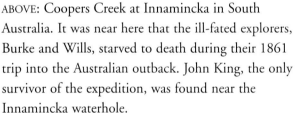

ABOVE: Coopers Creek at Innamincka in South Australia. It was near here that the ill-fated explorers, Burke and Wills, starved to death during their 1861 trip into the Australian outback. John King, the only survivor of the expedition, was found near the Innamincka waterhole.

ABOVE RIGHT: Countryside littered with old drays and rusting bits of equipment and a collection of ruins are all that remain of Farina in South Australia. Farina was a former service centre on the Ghan Railway Line linking Adelaide to Alice Springs.

RIGHT: Sunset on Lake Eyre in the remote desert lands of South Australia. Covering about 9300 square kilometres, this lake is the lowest part of the Australian continent, having sunk to 17 metres below sea level.

OPPOSITE: A few puddles are all that remain of a creek bed near Tibooburra, reputed to be the hottest place in New South Wales.

OVERLEAF: Combo Waterhole, situated on the Diamantina River in Queensland, is believed to be the site that inspired Banjo Paterson to write 'Waltzing Matilda' while on a visit to the nearby Dagworth Station in 1895.

ABOVE: Ruins of the Mulka Store, established in 1883 by Alexander Scobie to provide supplies for travellers on the mail trucks crossing the Birdsville Track. The 514 kilometre track goes from Marree in South Australia to Birdsville in Queensland.

ABOVE RIGHT: The Blanche Cup, a mound spring in Wabma Kadarbu Mound Springs Conservation Park. These springs are formed by water seeping to the surface from the Great Artesian Basin, a huge natural underground reservoir of water. Sand and minerals deposit to form mounds that rise above the surrounding flat, salty landscape. Lush green reeds and other plants grow around the spring, supporting a variety of bird and aquatic life.

CENTRE RIGHT AND RIGHT: The weathered rounded boulders of the Devil's Marbles balance precariously on top of one another beside the highway to Alice Springs, south of Tennant Creek. In Aboriginal mythology, these stones were said to be the eggs of the Rainbow Serpent.

LEFT: The Homestead Waterhole at Mungeranie, an oasis in the harsh country of the Birdsville Track, about halfway between Maree and Birdsville.

BELOW: The massive walls of King's Canyon in Watarrka National Park appear to be sliced through with a giant knife. The smooth face of this wall has been caused by huge slabs of rock breaking away evenly along vertical joint lines. Notable for the severity of its rock formations, the canyon is bordered by ancient sandstone walls rising 100 metres to a plateau of rocky domes and is the Red Centre's deepest and most striking gorge. The beautiful King's Canyon is called Watarrka by the Aboriginal people, after the acacia trees that grow there, and has been deserted for more than half a century, the memory of the people living on only in a few rock paintings at sites scattered throughout the park.

OPPOSITE AND CENTRE RIGHT: Rugged outback country near Winton in Queensland. This is the centre of the Matilda Country, a diverse, undulating region in which vast Mitchell grass plains are broken by magnificent coloured gorges, ridges and jump-ups. There is a wide variety of bird and animal life in the area, best seen at dawn or dusk.

BELOW: The Anzac Hill War Memorial at Alice Springs was unveiled on Anzac Day 1934 by RSL President and first post-master of Alice Springs, Dudley Adamson.

RIGHT: The town of Alice Springs, as seen from Billy Goat Hill. The second largest town in the Northern Territory, 'The Alice', as it is affectionately known, was once a vital link on the overland telegraph line and is now a popular destination for tourists exploring the nearby MacDonnell Ranges, Uluru and Kata Tjuta.

BOTTOM RIGHT: The historic telegraph station at Alice Springs was established in 1872 to relay messages between Darwin and Adelaide. It was one of twelve stations along the Overland Telegraph Line. The original stone buildings have been restored with house furnishings and artifacts from the early 1900s and are open to the public.

OPPOSITE: The late afternoon light on sand dunes near Merty Merty in outback South Australia reveals the dramatic patterns made by the prevailing winds.

ABOVE: The McDouall Range in Tennant Creek is also known as the Honeymoon Range, so-named because two miners brought their new brides to live there. The rich gold and copper fields of this area gave rise to famous mines like Peko, named after a prospector's dog. Hundreds of old mines are still to be found in this range.

BELOW: The long abandoned Curdimurka railway siding between the old Ghan Railway Line and the Oodnadatta Track. For many years this siding was home to the many fettlers who looked after the railway between Marree and William Creek. The site had already fallen into disrepair long before the line was closed in 1980.

ABOVE: Ruins at Farina, once the railhead for loading cattle and a meeting place for Afghan cameleers on the Oodnadatta Track. The Oodnadatta Track, a dirt road from Marree through to Oodnadatta, follows a major Aboriginal trade route, the original track taken by the explorer John McDouall Stuart, the Overland Telegraph Line and the Old Ghan Railway.

CENTRE: The old railway station at Oodnadatta, which was proclaimed a town in 1890. It became a mecca for drovers and the teamsters from the top half of the continent and a depot for the desert camel caravans.

BELOW: Strangways siding on the Oodnadatta Track. Built in 1872, the Telegraph Repeater Station was once the hub of a tiny community and the ruins are now under State Heritage Listing.

OPPOSITE: The Old Peake Telegraph Station and Homestead ruins, on the Oodnadatta Track. This was once a major centre for the Overland Telegraph Line. It was also the base for explorer Ernest Giles on his western surveys and supported a small copper mining community in the early 1900s.

LEFT: Spinifex grass dots the Gibson Desert in Central Australia. Covering almost half the continent, the deserts of Australia are extremely diverse in appearance, ranging from endless, undulating red sand dunes to flat, stony gibber plains. Few areas are entirely barren, with spinifex, tussocky grasses, mulga, mallee and small scrub lightly clothing the landscape.

BELOW: Henbury Meteorite Conservation Park is the site of a number of meteorite craters, the largest of which have left depressions in the ground measuring 180 metres across and 15 metres deep. Scientists estimate that a meteorite made up of nickel and iron crashed into the area about 7400 years ago. The Aboriginal people have a legend that the craters were formed during a fiery explosion and call the place 'Chindu china waru chingi yabu' which means 'Sun walk fire devil rock'.

ABOVE LEFT: Scorched, cracked earth in the outback of South Australia. Covering almost 60 million hectares, this is one of the most remote regions in the world, where conditions are severe, climate harsh and distances overwhelming.

CENTRE LEFT: The memorial to John Flynn, founder of the Royal Flying Doctor Service and the Australian Inland Mission is in the West MacDonnell Ranges, west of Alice Springs. The service provides aeromedical emergency and primary health care together with communication and education assistance to those who live, travel and work in regional and remote places of Australia.

LEFT: The Gunbarrel Highway, an isolated desert track of 1400 kilometres from Wiluna to Yalara, was the first of a series of roads built by surveyor Len Beadell and was completed in 1958. The roads were cut to provide service access to the Woomera Rocket Range.

ABOVE: The jagged, red rock cliffs of the Glen Helen Gorge in the West MacDonnell Ranges are formed from quartzite. Once a huge inland sea, sandstone was deposited in the area 500 million years ago. It was subsequently tilted and uplifted, with the Finke River slowly eroding its way through the mountain range.

TOP LEFT: Aboriginal artist Albert Namatjira's (1902–1954) monument stands sentinel over the MacDonnell Ranges. Namatjira, one of Australia's greatest national and international artists, drew inspiration from the vibrant colours of the surrounding countryside. He became famous as the first Aboriginal artist of the desert to lead the move into contemporary media and to paint landscapes in a European fashion, breaking away from the traditional art of his people, the Western Aranda. He and his wife were the first Aborigines to be granted Australian citizenship.

LEFT: Salt patterns on the desert in the Wabma Kadarbu Conservation Park. Desert country surrounding the salt-encrusted Lake Eyre has been used for grazing. Bores have been sunk to use the artesian water which is too saline for human consumption but can be used for stock and some domestic purposes.

LEFT: Blanche Cup and The Bubbler, two mound springs fed from the Great Artesian Basin in Wabma Kadarbu Conservation Park, provide an important water source in a very arid environment.

LEFT: Gibber and grass-covered plains dominate the eastern part of Sturt National Park, 340 000 hectares of semi-desert country in the far western corner of New South Wales. The park protects a diversity of landscape from the red sand dunes of the Strzelecki desert to wetlands, flat-topped mesas, remant gidgee woodland, the catchment system of the ephemeral Twelve-Mile Creek and 450 million year old granite tors.

OPPOSITE: Mesas and steep escarpments display magnificent earthy colours in breakaway country in Sturt National Park.

OPPOSITE: The Breakaways, north of Coober Pedy, are a stunning example of mesa and stony gibber desert scenery. Movies of world acclaim such as *Mad Max—Beyond Thunderdome*, *Priscilla Queen of the Desert* and *Pitch Black* have been filmed in this region. Over 70 million years ago a vast inland sea covered this area, which is rich in Aboriginal and European history.

TOP RIGHT: Chambers Pillar rises 34 metres above the plain in the Chambers Pillar Historical Reserve south of Alice Springs. First recorded in 1860 by John McDouall Stuart, who likened it to 'a locomotive engine with its funnel', the pillar is the remnant of a mesa in its final stages of decay. In a Dreamtime legend the pillar is a spirit ancestor who took a woman from a forbidden totemic group. The couple were exiled with the man becoming the pillar and the woman the largest of the nearby castle-like hills.

RIGHT: Dawn silhouettes the head of an opal mine at Coober Pedy. Opal was first found here in 1915 and the area now supplies the world with the majority of gem quality opal. With temperatures rising to 50°C in summer, about 80 per cent of the population of Coober Pedy live underground. It is claimed that the first people to live underground were miners who had been soldiers in Europe during World War I. Used to living in trenches they knew the climatic advantages gained from living in the constant temperature of a dugout.

RIGHT: Keeping in touch with civilisation—signpost at William Creek on the Oodnadatta Track, one of the most isolated towns in the South Australian outback.

RIGHT: Sunset over the Chambers Pillar Historical Reserve. This landmark was very important in guiding the region's earliest pioneers.

OVERLEAF: White trunked river gums contrast with red rock walls at Ellery Gorge in the MacDonnell ranges, west of Alice Springs.

ABOVE: Rising high above the desert plain, the 28 great rock domes of Kata Tjuta are venerated by the Aborigines as 'the many-headed one'. Covering an area of 35 square kilometres, they create a stunning silhouette against the sky. The rocks are made up of pebbles and boulders of granite, gneiss and volcanic rocks, which were torn away from the mountain by the sea and then rolled smooth before finally being cemented together by a fine sandstone. The resulting rock type is known as 'conglomerate'.

BELOW LEFT: The Todd River after rain. The river, which runs through the town of Alice Springs is dry except after flash floods. Each year it is the venue for a 'dry' race, a quirky event in which the competitors run on the bed of the river carrying home-made replicas of harbour yachts.

BELOW RIGHT: Arid, inhospitable sand dune country in outback South Australia, near William Creek.

OPPOSITE: A welcome creek bed, west of Carnegie Homestead. Here, in the centre of Western Australia, the Gunbarrel Highway degenerates into harsh gravel tracks with numerous creek crossings.

OPPOSITE: Old fenceline at the Carnegie Homestead at the western end of the Gunbarrel Highway in Western Australia. Herd management in this part of the world is fraught with difficulties. Paddocks are vast, with one of the holding paddocks here being enclosed by 32 kilometres of fenceline.

ABOVE: Remains of the Dalhousie Homestead, built in the 1880s. More than a century of sheep and cattle grazing ceased in this area when it was declared Witjira National Park in 1985.

CENTRE RIGHT: For thousands of years before European discovery, the Dalhousie Springs in Witjira National Park provided water, shelter, food and medicines for the desert Aborigines. The springs are home to unique species of fish such as the Lake Eyre hardyhead.

BOTTOM RIGHT: Purnie Bore in Witjira National Park. The park covers 7770 square kilometres on the western edge of the Simpson Desert in the far north of South Australia.

ABOVE: The Simpson Desert, Witjira National Park. With an annual rainfall of less than 125 millimetres, this area is one of the driest parts of the continent. In 1845 explorer Charles Sturt was the first European to view the 170 000 square kilometre desert but it was not named until the 1930s when explorer and geologist, Cecil Thomas Madigan, named it after Allen Simpson, the sponsor of his subsequent expedition. The largest sand dunes occur in this desert. Running in a north–south direction, they extend up to 300 kilometres in length and reach 40 metres in height.

CENTRE LEFT AND BOTTOM LEFT: After rains, the dry inland areas of Australia become alive with a colourful kaleidoscope of wildflowers. Mid-west Western Australia is some of the world's best wildflower country with a magical parade of colour brightening the landscape from June to November.

OPPOSITE: Relics from farming days at the Mount Dare homestead. Formerly a cattle station, Mount Dare is today part of Witjira National Park in South Australia.

LEFT: State emblem of South Australia, the striking Sturt's desert pea *(Clianthus formosus)* colours dry inland Australia after the rains in spring and summer. It was first discovered by explorer William Dampier in 1688 when he visited islands off the coast of north-western Australia. It was named after Captain Charles Sturt who noted the presence of this plant in 1844 while exploring between Adelaide and Central Australia. An annual, it is found mostly in Central Australia and further south to northern South Australia.

BELOW: Desert wildflowers near Cue in Western Australia. In this outback environment white, gold and pink everlastings flourish along with billy buttons, purple vetch, flannel bush, daisies, wild pansies, mulla mulla, acacia, lamb's tails, poverty bush, parakeelya and blue pincushion.